ONLY TWO
(SEEMS LIKE MORE)

Susan Sturgill

Susan Sturgill
12/9/94

The Laughing Academy Press
P.O. Box 02061 Columbus OH 43202

Requests for permission should be submitted to Susan Sturgill, Laughing Academy Press, P.O. Box 02061, Columbus, OH 43202

ISBN 09626108-4-4

Manufactured in the U.S.A. Printed and bound by Worzalla Publishing Co. for The Laughing Academy Press in a first edition of 2500 copies April 1, 1990. Second printing September 23, 1992.

For Claire

"By associating with the cat, one only risks becoming richer."

— Colette
The Tendrils of the Vine

In grateful acknowledgement of

Kitty	Mr. White
Sonny	Brownie
Simon I	Butch
Simon II	Jane
Schuster	Izzy
Ernest	Moe

Valentine

The Essence of Felinicity

Couch Potato and Meatloaves

Cats enjoy the occasional evening of mindless entertainment.....

...but they prefer an educational nature program.

Cats like to stay on top of current events

Cats do not approve of smoking

Cats hate cleaning.....

nature abhors a vacuum.

.... because it disturbs the arrangement of their toys.

Before Cleaning

Cleaning

Ten minutes after cleaning...

Cats like to hang out.

MIGHTY HUNTER

HIS PREY

BALLOON

GRASSHOPPER

SOCKS

STRING

RUBBER BAND

FEATHER

LEAF

The cat's reasoning faculties are very highly developed...

EEEK

* What time do you start serving breakfast?

* I want to go to Miami.

Family Outing

Packaging

The Cat and the Baby: Chapter I — Breakfast Envy

Morning Thunder

Cats do not understand the appeal of full immersion bathing.

The morning grooming ritual

Cats Like to Help

There's no question about the advantages of a personal trainer

Cats become seriously concerned when they see otherwise sane people take to exercise equipment.

A CATALOG OF HOME OFFICE ACCESSORIES

Kitten on the keys

Did you say "mouse"

printer monitor

Cats like to make houseguests feel welcome.

Dusting those hard-to-reach places

Tidying clutter

Bedmaking

Dishwashing

Cats excel at housekeeping

Laundry

Cat Dancing Lesson #12:

THE MEXICAN CAT DANCE

At no time do the feet touch the cat.... The cat remains motionless....

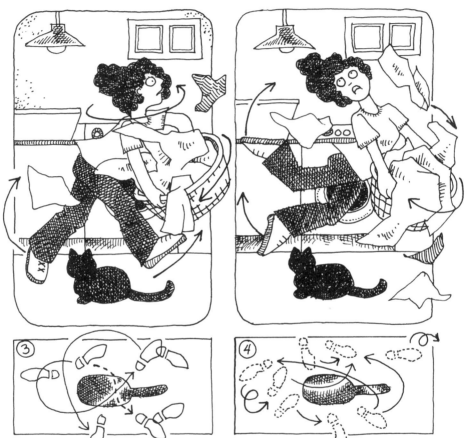

The laundry creates a dramatic effect... Facial expression is important! You: alarmed. The cat: oblivious....

Grand Finale.

The man who loved cat dancing →

Cats Just Want to Have Fun

Teenage Ninja Cats

Cats _love_ Christmas

—George Herriman